I Have Found a Song

Enitharmon Editions

I Have Found

Poems and images about enslavement to mark
the Bicentenary of the Abolition of the Slave Trade Act

a Song

First published in 2010 by
Enitharmon Editions
26b Caversham Road
London NW5 2DU

www.enitharmon.co.uk

Poems and images © The poets and artists 2010
Text on *Human Cargo* © Marco Livingstone 2010

ISBN 978-1-904634-87-4 (de luxe)
ISBN 978-1-904634-86-7 (regular)

The origins of *I Have Found a Song*

In 2007–8, Arts Council England supported a wide range of artists and arts organisations commemorating the Bicentenary of the Abolition of the Slave Trade Act. As part of this activity, the Arts Council itself commissioned a new piece of work, on the theme of enslavement, from each of eleven poets, with a twelfth poem chosen from a competition open to the general public. One at a time, the poems were published on the Arts Council website, with the set of all twelve poems being completed by the addition of the competition winner in April 2008. Subsequently, five artists were invited by Enitharmon Editions to contribute the images reproduced in this book, including original prints specially commissioned for the *de luxe* edition.

At Arts Council England, Samenua Sesher and John Hampson initiated the project, commissioned the poets, and asked Enitharmon Editions to coordinate publication of the words and images. Samenua was Director of decibel, an Arts Council England initiative which sought to support and raise the profile of artists of African, Asian and Caribbean descent in England. Comprising a cross art-form programme of projects and events, decibel was launched in 2003 and ran until March 2008.

Acknowledgements

Special thanks are due to Samenua Sesher and John Hampson, who initiated this project, and to the writers and artists who have so enthusiastically participated in it.

We are also most grateful for the work of the book designer Peter Willberg; the etching and lithographic printers Mike Taylor and Simon Marsh of Paupers Press; Ted Chau of Chaudigital; and the art historian Marco Livingstone for his enlightening note on Paula Rego's *Human Cargo*.

We have also received help from the following: Tessa Jackson of Iniva at Rivington Place; Indra Khanna; Martha Lineham of the Bridgeman Art Library; Marie-Anne McQuay and Nemia MacLachlan of Spike Island, Bristol; Mary Miller and Frankie Rossi of Marlborough Fine Art and Marlborough Graphics; Nilesh Mistry of Cartwright Hall Art Gallery, Bradford; Richard Riley of the British Council; Patrick Roe of The Fine Book Bindery; Kevin Smith of John Jones Art Centre; and Mara-Helen Wood of the University Gallery, Northumbria University.

Stephen Stuart-Smith

Contents

Patience Agbabi *The Shoe* 8

Polly Atkin *Seven Nights of Uncreation* 11

Sonia Boyce 12

Valerie Bloom *Legacy* 22

Jean 'Binta' Breeze *Dream Time* 24

Hew Locke 26

Fred D'Aguiar *Legal Tender* 30

Helen Dunmore *I owned a woman once* 33

Shanti Panchal 34

Bernardine Evaristo *What if* 39

Paul Farley *Cloaca Maxima* 40

Paula Rego 42

Jacob Sam-La Rose *Magnitude* 50

Iain Sinclair *Late History* 52

Chris Steele-Perkins 54

Hugo Williams *The Boy-Call* 60

Benjamin Zephaniah *An Interesting Visit* 62

Biographies 64
Colophon 66

Patience Agbabi *The Shoe*

1

The day the sun spilt red
on the sea and fat black clouds shed
monsoon rain, she split my head

open on sand and wrote her name –
Alishka, meaning *I am not to blame*.
Tiny child of my brain.

I lifted her body, purple as a bruise,
to my breast and she tasted the blues
of a mother who wears shame for shoes.

Then plump on pain she rode my back,
my belly concave with the lack
of a moon to pull the tide of fate back.

No pumpkin carriage to carry us through,
no prince to say *I do*,
only a passport if I wore the shoe

with the six-inch heel that winked in the sun,
kissed the lips and forked tongue
that hissed *Miss First World*. The deed is done.

Alishka is my world. But the world is small
and cannot grow if it doesn't go to school.
The day I flew I scattered my soul

on the beach and took a photograph
of Alishka in my head. Her baby laugh.
Her chubby grubby hands. Her hidden birthmark.

And for seven years I watched her baby face
becoming mine, her father's: my grimace,
his thin-lipped smile. From that place

they call the First World. Four walls of lies.
For a smile on the lips cannot disguise
dead eyes.

The day I flew the sun went out.
I slept in the bowels of the beast that cut
clouds into question marks. Barefoot,

I arrived and queued in a snake of many colours.
They questioned me so long I forgot who I was.
The face on my passport, Alishka's.

2

So this is your passport? she said
as she filed Sinda's fate. Her nails were red,

Sinda's were red raw. Two pounds an hour,
an hour that stretched to seven years hard labour.

Sinda is cook, clean, serve, clean.
Sinda = microwave, dishwasher, washing machine,

tumble drier, hoover. Sleep in the kitchen.
From six a.m. to two a.m, plugged in.

Sinda make white noise. Sinda on standby.
Sinda dial 00, hear a baby cry,

see a small girl writing in sand
2+2 = six. No magic wand

to wave when machine break
down. No money, no passport, no snake-

skin shoe with heel to stab her mistress' heart,
reboot, kick start,

just running barefoot through snow with heels
so hard she doesn't know how freedom feels.

3

They said I had claws for toes.
They said if you wear no shoes
you're nobody. It does

not matter how I flew back to my brain,
that I aged twenty years in shame,
or how the village spat my name.

All I wished was to see the girl in my head
who wrote her name on sand in blood
yet never learnt to read.

Alishka! I cried. The young girl stared.
Her heels winked in the sun, her toenails red.
You are not my mummy, she said.

Polly Atkin *Seven Nights of Uncreation*

On the first night I woke up deep underwater,
dry as a fish-bone in the belly of a ship,
the heavy silence below the water-line
punctured by crackings like timbers or bones
smashing to splinters on unseen rocks.
I was blind, trapped. Utterly lost.

On the second a glimmer of pinkish light
showed pillars rising from lengthening sides
to meet in the curve of the ceiling like arches.
Something within me could tell without asking
that these were the ribs of a monstrous creature,
the platform I stood on, its lung.

On the third night the taste of the dark was different;
I felt right at once I was deep underground
with the weight of the wet earth driving me down,
the metallic blood-tang of hewn rock in my mouth
and a prescient knowledge I'd never get out.
I was buried, the cave was a tomb.

By the fourth night of this I was wary of dreams,
the days between blinking, plagued by impressions
I did not recall from the nights' haunting visions,
but knew from their otherness they were the same.
I arrived just like home on a wide open plain,
but the wind spoke in alien tongues.

On the fifth night I rose to the ridge of a hill,
my eyes fixed by chance to a passage below,
where a sad slow procession wound its way north
into shadow, hung over the land like a hawk.
I felt it important to watch, but the wind
and the rain relieved me of sight.

On the sixth night I fell into nothing. Nothing
smothered me, crushing and crowding around,
everywhere, blankness rubbing me out
inch by inch, until I was nothing. I stuttered,
coughed when I tried to speak.
When I tried to scream I was mute.

The seventh night was a night of rest.
I crouched awake till the birds' dawn chorus,
hearing them singing to hours of darkness,
thinking *I'm them; I am just like the birds,*
tricked into ludicrous song by illusion,
tricked to believe in the false dawn light.

On the dawn of the eighth day I unlocked my limbs,
and stepped into a new life.

Sonia Boyce

Is this love that I'm feeling?

For many years now, I have been using words (names, quotes, lyrics) as the starting point for making simple, but meditative drawings, where the drawing activity involves copying and tracing – following the contours of the previous lines.

'Is this love that I'm feeling?' is one of my favourite songs by Bob Marley, who has been a major influence on a generation seeking to find a way out of the legacies of slavery and colonialism. Despite the seductive confidence of 'Is this love that I'm feeling?', the lyrics suggest emotional vulnerability. As ever, I am attracted to the bitter sweet.

Sonia Boyce

Is this love that I'm feeling?, 2009–10
Etching, 39.5 × 49 cm
Included in *de luxe* edition of *I Have Found a Song*

Crop Over: a project by Sonia Boyce (2007)

Crop Over is a carnival that takes place in Barbados. Unlike most Pre-Lenten carnivals it comes directly from the conditions of slavery and sugar production on the plantations. My understanding of Crop Over developed when I encountered folk characters like the Mother Sally, Donkey Man, Shaggy Bear and Stilt Walker.

Crop Over: a project by Sonia Boyce (2007) also responds to the history of Harewood House, owned by the Lascelles family in England, and its relationship to the Transatlantic Slave Trade. The Lascelles family association with Barbados started in the seventeenth century when Edward Lascelles and his son Daniel were based in Bridgetown, Barbados.

In 2007, with the assistance of the National Art Gallery Committee, Barbados and Harewood House, I went to Barbados to make a film and find out more about Crop Over and its connection with the UK. These photographs, video stills, and interviews with cultural historians and the performers who play the characters, form part of that project.

There's a tradition in the Anglophone Caribbean of fife and drum. Fife: meaning flute, penny whistle, and a bass and small kettle drum. Several islands have it. In Barbados, that tradition has come to be represented by what we call a Tuk Band. We're not sure why Tuk? There have been stories of it being a Scottish word, but that's never been fully established.

Photo: Sonia Boyce
Text: Dr Marcia Burrowes

SONIA BOYCE

It is the music of the plantations, it's the music of the tenantries and the villages. The characters dance to this music, the masquerade characters of Donkey Man, Stilt Walkers, etc.

Photo: William St James Cummins
Text: Dr Marcia Burrowes

Shaggy Bear is a colourful Bajan character, and like all Bajan characters comes from Africa.

Shaggy Bear is an Orisha, or Legba. And, as an Orisha God, enters ceremonies first to clear it – literally and spiritually – so that the invited ancestors, other Orishas, can enter peacefully.

Shaggy Bear in Barbados is colourful and appears at local events, and to most people is just fun and flair.

SONIA BOYCE

"I am the Mother Sally" "I am the Mother Sally"

Photo: William St James Cummins
Text: Suzanne Watts & Troy King

Donkey Man goes back a long way. It could be British. It could be African. But this being a folk festival, and the people involved in it and planning it are the poor working-class people. So they used the donkey, which was symbolic of them, and the 'donkey-work' they had to do on the plantations.

Photo: William St James Cummins
Text: Peggy McGeary

This was another dance, this was another form of entertainment. The head of the donkey and its body was made out of wood, and a person would stand in the middle of it and dance. They held on to it and danced around, with the donkey rearing up and doing all sorts. Pretty much like what we see today. And people would run and pull at it, and you would take the donkey and attack them. There was this nice relationship between the Donkey Man and the crowd.

Valerie Bloom *Legacy*

If any man be found stealing any of his brethren and maketh merchandise of him, or selleth him, then the thief shall die, and thou shalt put away evil from among you. DEUT. 24:7

1

They have taken my voice, Mother,
And I am dumb,
No sound springs from my parted lips,
No groan or sigh,
No croak or curse
Or blessings fall.
Silence is all.

They have taken my name, Mother,
I am unknown,
If you should call I'll not respond,
Names pass me by unharnessed
Kwabena, Kwame,
Kofi, Kai,
Who am I?

They have taken my song, mother,
I cannot sing,
The melodies of home are silenced now,
No drums, no flutes,
No whistles wail,
No koras croon
A soulful tune.

They have taken my children, mother,
What use my rage?
Their piping cries still haunt my dreams,
Unused cups taunt,
The empty mat
Still mocks my gaze
Through ceaseless days.

They want my thoughts, mother,
But my face is blank,
I do not show distress or joy,
No twitch of jaw,
Nor curl of lip
No chains, they'll find,
Around my mind.

2

My fathers, I have made a voice,
I have replaced the one I lost.
From abandoned words and sounds
I fashioned it,
Tried it for size.
My fathers, I can vocalize!

My fathers, I have bought a name,
It does not wrap around the tongue
Like kente cloth around the waist,
But slips from lips
Like an eel through the hand,
I wear this name like an armband.

My fathers, I have found a song,
It wails high-pitched with sound of steel,
It dances from the skins of goats,
It sighs from guitar and banjo,
With syncopated beat I sing.
My fathers, I am surviving.

My fathers, I have found my sons,
My daughters, they're in every state,
From billboards they smile down at me,
They lead, they rule, they guide, they teach,
They call the world their home,
My fathers, we have overcome.

Jean 'Binta' Breeze *Dream Time*

Come to me softly in the night, my child
Come to me in my dreams
Come to me when my tears subside
And night can claim its sleep

I left you awake
In the early morn
To hunt for your naming day
For the feast we had planned in the village
And skins for the drums we would play

I travelled further from home
Than I had ever been before
Because I wanted the best for you
I wanted the spirits to come

When I heard the horn
That warned me of strangers
I was in an unknown land
Believe me, my son,
I ran to get home
But I was held in the steel of their hands

I was chained and marched
To the edge of the sea
Where I was packed in the hold of a boat
Sick and worn
I lost track of time
Till we arrived in this new found land
Now I work with my naked back to the sun
And the whips that crack my skin
The leaves of the cane are long and sharp
As we work from dawn into evening

Then comes the only peace, my son
A peace that waters my eyes
When I think of you
In your mother's arms
Thinking I must have died

The sunset comes around our shacks
And the fires cook our food
And I think of our village and my own land
And the tribe I left behind

So come to me softly in the night, my child,
Come to me in my dreams
Come to me when my tears subside
And night can claim its sleep

Many suns have set
Since I've been gone
And I think of how you've grown
Do you walk now
Do you talk now
Do you spell out your name
The one I chose for you
The one that told of the day you were born

Do you call for mama in the night
Do you still suckle on her breast
Does she whisper stories about me
Before she puts you down to rest

My first thoughts in the morning are about you
The way we would have played in the grass
I would have taken you to the river
I would have taught you how to swim
I would have made for you small arrows
And taught you how to hunt
I would have watched you growing tall and strong
As you would run to meet me in the evening

But now my days are broken
The machete scars my hands
A river's sweat pours off me
The sunlight has me blind

I've lost all hope of returning
I can't follow the trail across the sea

Sometimes in the darkening evening
I climb up the hill
And sit there looking out
How far away I am
I do not know

And even when my thoughts turn to running
To the mountains that I see up above
I know you won't be there, my son
I know you won't be there
There'll be no welcoming arms of your mother

So I stay here and brave the whips
Brave the hatred of the overseer
Brave the soil of the land we have to dig
But at least I can still be near the sea

Drinking in the spirits of the cane
Knowing my dreams are in vain

So stay close to home, my son
Do not go far when you hunt
These are the thoughts in my head
As I watch the sun dip a bloody red

Oh my son, how I want you to be free

So come to me softly in the night, my child
And I will come to you in your dreams
Come to me when the tears subside
And night can claim its sleep

Hew Locke

Lost World, 2009–10
Lithograph, 49 × 39.5 cm
Included in *de luxe* edition of *I Have Found a Song*

Lost World

The design incorporates a South African share certificate once owned by Sir Henry Rider Haggard, the author of *King Solomon's Mines* and *She*, and one of the founders of the 'Lost World' literary genre. Indiana Jones is said to be based on his character Allan Quatermain, who also reappears as himself as a major character in Alan Moore's graphic novels *The League of Extraordinary Gentlemen*.

Rider Haggard's books inspired the 'Lost World' design of South Africa's Sun City, a fantastical and romanticised theme park – which includes ancient African ruins, actors playing natives in fake villages, and many giant stone elephants – a highly profitable tourist attraction. Created during the apartheid years as an illusion for whites, a Neverland, a fantasy Africa, it is now equally popular with black and African tourists. Michael Jackson visited several times in the 1990s, and was there presented with a lifetime achievement award by Nelson Mandela.

This certificate is part of the history of the Scramble for Africa. It demonstrates another aspect of our desire to believe in dream worlds – in this case the promise of future riches. Sun City and the African Land Investment Company are both searches for profit wrapped up in an African dream.

Hew Locke *Sin Eater*

Sin Eater is a spectacular heraldic wall piece addressing themes of culture, history and global commerce. Created of cord and plastic beads, it presents a coat of arms specific to Liverpool that interweaves a host of symbols, icons and imagery from other cultures.

Sin Eater spills down the Bluecoat Gallery's walls. Neptune, god of the sea, stands defiantly upon the backs of two attendant 'liver birds' who grasp skulls in their beaks as he urinates onto the head of the devil. With trident and sceptre in hand, he is regally winged with a pair of double-headed horned lions derived from the tapestry *The Triumph of Fortitude* in the Walker Art Gallery, one of my favourite pieces in Liverpool.

Neptune's headdress consists of representations of men from two of Liverpool's most famous families. At the very top sits a skeletal bust of Sir Foster Cunliffe (1755–1834), grandson of Foster Cunliffe (1682–1758), who was three times the Mayor of Liverpool, sponsor of the Bluecoat School and one of the city's wealthiest slave merchants in the 18th century. It is believed that Sir Foster Cunliffe was uneasy about the history of his family business and he tried to conceal the origin of his immoral fortune.

Beneath Cunliffe a heraldic shield depicts Andrew Barclay Walker, who founded the Walker Art Gallery in 1873 while he was in office as Mayor of Liverpool. He also contributed other large sums of money to charity and art and literature in Liverpool throughout his life. Here, the benefactor is being stuck with voodoo pins by two green monkeys. The monkeys are derived from George Stubbs's painting in the Walker Art Gallery called *Green Monkey*. I see the monkey as being trapped in his collection, a very sad and tragic character, absurdly holding a peach.

The sash across Neptune's body and again under his feet reads 'Deus Nobis Haec Otia Fecit', the City of Liverpool's motto, which translates as 'God has given us these days of peace'. Other significant symbols are the head forms on Neptune's trident and his legs. Based on historic designs of brass weights used by the Ashanti people of West Africa to weigh gold dust, these heads suggest the role of trade in the fortunes of Liverpool: trade in gold, but also in people. Foster Cunliffe is believed to have traded with the Ashanti for slaves, and he also traded with Benin and Upper Guinea. This work is designed to take away the sins of the fathers so they will not be visited upon the children. It is a protection charm. Two weeks after this charm was removed from the wall, a serious fire broke out in these newly renovated galleries.

Fred D'Aguiar *Legal Tender*

1

I wait so long
I stand so still
Swallows sit on my
Shoulders and wash
In the fonts at my neck
I carry rain
Two cups' worth
In the dippers of my
Clavicles
I have no energy
To shoo them from me
One pecks something
From the stubble on my
Priced and purchased chin
I look old before my
Time while my time
Makes me look
Preternaturally
Older than I should be
Both are not the same
One is a set of lines
Chiselled in my forehead
The other curlicues
My spine and spirit
Spirit is the negative
In this picture of me
What I store in the crook
Of my arms where

The natural light
Plunges into darkness
I send from my time
To yours
I want to blink
I wish to roll my shoulders
Stretch my arms
Empty my clavicles
Of what's pooled there
More than a pulse
In my neck
Less than a breath
Touch my dry eyes
With your fingers
Dipped in free rain

2

Old man's head
Grafted to young
Underfed body

All skin and sharp
Bones and not
Much gristle

Polished skin
Refracts light
Sinews harbor

Shadows that
Define how this
Freed slave owns

Less than his
Owner's name
How his body

Looks as if
An increase
In daylight

Might crumble its
Papyrus into
Weightless ash

So that we see
Not this man
In this light

Not a freed slave
But the heads
Of our parents

Planted on the
Round shoulders
Of our children

3

As ordered
I wash with soap
History's soap

Hot on my skin
Onion skin
Crackles off me

Soap wraps gun-
Powder into balm
Binds sulphur

I wash off layers
Of black for what's
White underneath

Then raw red
Till I shine
Tin-whistle-clean

Whistle hollowed
From my whitened
Skin-and-bones

Play something

Helen Dunmore   *I owned a woman once*

so glossy fleshed, so high-coloured
my blood swept in my veins
she was rich and heaped in the belly
as the Bible says
she was fertile as the banks of a river
when the flood falls and the mud makes food,

I clothed her as I wanted to clothe her
I housed her as I wanted to house her
I put food on her plate to fatten her,

I owned a woman once so high-coloured
so dark and rich in the eyes
my blood would not be still in my veins
my eyes would not stop watching her –
a callous on her heel made my belly quiver –

I put food on her plate to fatten her
I put oil on her hair
she was fertile as the bank of a river,

I owned a woman once so high-coloured
so slow and sure in her walk
that all eyes walked with her,
I owned her from broken toenail
to breath that misted my mirror

and I clothed her as I wanted to clothe her,
her flesh hidden, her body shrouded
while she fattened with my child,

yes, mostly it was sweet to own her
but sometimes I had to punish her
for her eyes everywhere looking
for the moist folds of her body hidden
and the rich darkness of her eyes looking.

Soon it came to her time
and this woman I owned lay on the ground
in the room I kept for her
with the midwife I paid for her
but her belly would not release the child

And the cage of her hips would not let go the child.
The midwife said she came to it too young
maybe, this woman I owned

but believe me
she was straight out of the Bible
so glossy-fleshed, so high-coloured
so heaped and rich in the belly
with one bare callous on her heel.

Shanti Panchal

Handkerchief Seller, 2010
Ink-jet print, 49 × 39.5 cm
Originally made as a watercolour, 1982
Included in *de luxe* edition of *I Have Found a Song*

Handkerchief Seller (1982)

This painting was derived from my time spent in Mumbai while I was studying there. It was fascinating to see the energy and struggle for survival in this big cosmopolitan city: people selling literally anything they could get their hands on, to sustain themselves and their families. While walking from Victoria Terminus railway station (now called Chhatrapati Shivaji Terminus) to the art school Sir J. J. School of Art every day, I observed this woman selling handkerchiefs in her upside-down umbrella on the footpath. Her muted colour sari, her worn-out feet, scattered newspaper nearby and her conditioned harsh reality were all visible on her sunburnt face. This was a striking visual experience for me.

(left) *First Marriage*, 1986
Watercolour on paper, 102 × 76 cm
© Bradford Art Galleries and Museums/The Bridgeman Art Library

(right) *Trading Things*, 2007
Watercolour on paper, 56 × 38 cm
Collection of the artist

First Marriage (1986)

There is an autobiographical element which runs in my work. This painting is about my arranged marriage in the village (in western India where I grew up) when I was about 15 years old. Instead of being a happy and joyous event, it's full of sadness. Although the young couple's garments are knotted together, no two figures could look more apart. The other family members in the painting have a look of immense sadness. This is how I had felt at the time when I did not wish to get married at that early age, as I had an aspiration to go to an art school in Mumbai and become an artist, although I had no idea at that time what being an artist really meant.

Trading Things (2007)

I went to see a friend in Wembley. While waiting at the reception, I observed a young lady carrying several pink boxes come to the reception. One could hardly see her behind the boxes. The expression on her face was withdrawn and overworked – some traces of enslavement, I suppose. I did not have an opportunity to talk about her predicament, to discover the circumstances she found herself in. I found it interesting to see the figure, the dark coloured head hemmed in between the yellowish wall and the pile of pink boxes. But this is how sometimes such an ordinary encounter expresses a deeper side of universal experience.

Bernardine Evaristo *What if*

Kidnapped from my village in Sunderland
by Scottish warlords out to make a fast buck.

Shipped across the ocean to Okondo State,
to labour in the mines until my lungs packed up.

Stripped of my name – Elizabeth Jones (16 ½)
I was given a new one – Bakamamendere.

Forbidden to speak my native tongue – Ing!ish,
I was force-fed their click one – Man!do!ng!ala.

Banned from worship of my One True God,
I prayed to their numerous deities instead.

I became the original *babymudder*, of course.
My job description? To increase the work force.

I soon learnt my pink skin was just like a pig's,
my indecent body hair resembled a primate's.

Yes! You people are animals: Beheadings (Check),
Countless wars (Check), *Genocide* (Check mate).

Because your brains are smaller than ours (Fact),
you cannot curb your savage instincts.

Because I listened for centuries without right of reply,
when I tried to object I came over as tongue-tied,

or – with a 'chip on my shoulder', and sometimes –
as violent: my gun turned against my own.

Paul Farley *Cloaca Maxima*

I

Sewer-jumping in a childhood twilight
the boy looks up a moment and feels something.
Water thick as Bovril doesn't move.
There's a holding of the breath in a concrete outfall.
It's an ear-to-the-rail moment,
or pipe-work, leading back to God-knows-where,
before an iron door slams shut on the splendours.

II

Moment containing all the fine escapees
of history, crawling through the dark, emerging
from unmarked graves aligned to navigations
they dug and died alongside. One long chain gang
raised from tobacco fields unlocked from work-songs
they sung in warmer, thicker air – *If you*
Don't believe I'm a sinkin, look what a hole I'm in –
the blistered of the Dismal Swamp Canal
who've travelled via the Underground Railroad
and Anacharsis Cloots – what's he doing here? –
with Representatives of the Human Race
all covered in shit, blinking in the light of day,
the shut-in, nameless multitudes, the lost bones,
the leg-irons and the long shanks and the ledger-
entered of Goree Island: all raised up!

III

Look at these three, marching through the visible field
from left to right, a ragged and sooty sentence
in the buttery, limestone light, in the middle of a century.
Marching into three futures long since past.

The little one says to the big one: *Who is this bloke?*
in a lost vernacular of Parisian sweeps
which the camera couldn't record. To which the big one
replies: *Never mind. Keep looking straight ahead*

though he's secretly intrigued. The apparatus
is a little like when a chimney grate's sealed off
by a canvas rig. And how many days has he seen
as a pinprick at the end of a carbon flue?

The middle one has climbed towards this light
so many times already in his short life,
and you want to tell him how long he's lasted in it
where so many others are shut in the dusty dark.

IV

Or think in terms of a movie shot
on a shoestring, where the eye is drawn
to the extras who are swapping hats
and passing by again and again.

Only replace its flimsy set
with sewers and ditches and holes in the ground,
and a scene that lasts millions of feet;
and the background babble with the sound

of a bullwhip that reverberates
down dark tunnels, and the same faces
come round eventually if you wait
for a few lifetimes and remain in your places.

V

The sleepers' hands are put to work.
Workhouse children unsnarl looms
and sharecroppers shuck peas from pods
and cocklers rake through dark mortar
and cotton pickers twist the buds
and bonded women solder boards
and run the fabric through the foot
and guide it down the miles of seam
and punkah wallahs pull the cord
and galley rowers bend through oars
and railroad workers tap the rails
and drainage diggers heft the spade
and all of this and so much more
is happening in the place of dreams.
The sleepers' hands are put to work.

VI

And this is what the boy has seen: the dreams
kept hidden, either by great distances
or the pearlescent blind eye that we need
to grow to keep the world under our noses
safely removed. The millions of mixed shades
are still running beneath our surfaces
and visible to those who just step sideways
anywhere: a city square at dusk,
a sun-warmed wall asking to have an ear
lent to its crumbling roughcast, old outfalls
like this one, where a boy gave way to thought
thirty years ago, on a backfield, in the north.

Paula Rego

Death Goes Shopping, *Penetration* and *Little Brides with their Mother* are three etchings that I conceived together, telling the same story. I dreamt the idea up, but I drew everything from a set I made. I had been to see an exhibition on the grotesque in Antwerp, and there they have the most beautiful lace dresses you can imagine. I went into a shop and there were all these children's dresses in white. I bought a lot of them. It struck me that they were like little bridal gowns, and when I got back to my studio in London I made some dolls and put them in these dresses. I made up a story that they were kept in chains and that they were going to be sold: marketed young and loaded on a cart, like chickens, by a nasty woman representing Death. That way they can grow up married to whoever they're going to be sold to. It's as simple as that: it's just children being marketed. In one of the pictures Death isn't present but the mother is there instead, looking very sad, with a little girl crying. They will soon get used to it.

When you sell a horse, you put your hand inside the mouth to check the teeth and establish its worth. That's what the woman is doing in *Penetration*, to see that the child is all right for selling. The children are in chains, and they're very small because they're little brides. They sell them as brides, very young. I always imagine everything in my pictures happening in Portugal, where I grew up. There was a fair we had there every year, which I always went to, and I can imagine these girls being sold in the fair, like beasts. When you take your chickens or whatever it is to the fair, you put them in cages. People come along and inspect them. And this is the same, except they're not in cages, they're just contained by the platform. Each person comes along and picks one, then another one.

Little Brides with their Mother shows the end of the story. The horrible Death has eaten the others and the mother is left with the children to suffer without Death pushing her. It's Death's job, isn't it, to do this sort of thing?

Paula Rego

Death Goes Shopping, 2009–10
2-plate etching with aquatint, 39.5 × 49 cm
Included in *de luxe* edition of *I Have Found a Song*

PAULA REGO

Penetration, 2009–10
Etching, 39.5 × 49 cm

Little Brides with their Mother, 2009–10
Etching, 39.5 × 49 cm

PAULA REGO

Human Cargo, 2007–08
Graphite, conté crayon and wash on paper
Triptych: 137 × 102 cm, 163 × 163 cm, 137 × 102 cm
Collection of the artist

Jacob Sam-La Rose *Magnitude*

when I say 'night',
it is your name I am calling,
when I say 'field',
your thousand, thousand names,
your million names.

ARACELIS GIRMAY, 'ARROZ POETICA'

I

There are a million grains in a 20 kilogram sack of rice.
Give or take. It's a hard enough number to imagine,

the kind that slips through the fingers, like digging
your hands in that same sack, trying to feel

for individuals; the kind of number that surpasses
counting, bigger than the mind's computational eye,

like the full, unending girth of sky, like death,
the kind of threshold you give up on

and take for granted. Imagine the sum
in eleven of those sacks, and I'm trying to find a way

to make that number real, like how many pots and how long
it might take to cook that much rice, and still retain the detail

of each swollen grain; a real, fleshy equation that might capture
the percentage of wastage, the amount that would fall

and be forgotten even while trying to keep count,
the appetite that might be necessary to take it all in.

Paula Rego *Human Cargo*

The large-scale drawings on the theme of human trafficking and honour killings made by Paula Rego in 2007–8 refer to everyday martyrdoms that were widely reported in the British press. We view the suffering of young women either at the hands of the very families that should be caring for them or at the behest of those who had treacherously promised them a better life only to condemn them to a hellish existence of prostitution, beatings and enslavement. The pictures themselves are sufficiently explicit for it to be unnecessary to spell out in the titles what barbarous acts are taking place. The imposing triptych in which the series culminates finds the entire cast of characters packed claustrophobically together into crates, making explicit their treatment as mere commodities.

Rego draws attention in *Human Cargo* to the various predicaments in which women of all ages may find themselves. The little girl resting wearily on a rucksack in the foreground of a central panel is already turning into an old woman: having been sent away to school at the age of just three, she learned early how to endure the loneliness of solitary confinement. Behind her an obese elderly blind woman is left abandoned as she approaches death. The grandmother is so old that nobody now will buy her. The younger women, more attractive to potential customers, have been packed up for sale, pressed against a surrogate draped figure whose pendulous appendages are there to instruct them in the sexual acts to which they are soon to be subjected. These are harrowing scenes eliciting both our compassion and our anger that even in the 21st century human beings should continue to be stripped of their dignity, robbed of their independence and freedom and subjected to a destiny of captivity and despair.

Marco Livingstone

II

In a lesson on trying to make the abstract more concrete,
one of my students, a Guyanese boy, late teens,

shares a draft in which he's counting
the breaths of a sleeping girlfriend.

He's met her father, shook his hand;
weeks later, the girl explains

that her Akan blood arrows back up to royalty,
that the boy is the son of a slave,

that there is no future for them, only a past.
I understand that the counting makes it easier,

lends a sense of a narrative, a march into the future
of something as simple as breath, in the face of something

so large it blots whatever light he'd been drawn by,
but it's not working, and as much as I try,

I can't suggest anything to make the poem any easier,
until he offers his own resolution: a memory

of sitting on the sea wall in Georgetown, facing the Atlantic,
following the darts of sunlight riding the backs of waves,

wondering where each began, how each follows
the heels of another as they furl

towards wall or shore, how he can only understand
as much of it as his eye can drink in,

how the rest, for him, is a mystery.

Iain Sinclair *Late History*

1

'Yes, there is a democracy based on slavery.
That's the Greek model. That works pretty well too…'
ED DORN

Sliding after night-storm to lose footing
on rake of wet-shingle, and stopped
by broken spar, tarry black in blood-varnish,
bitter nails of old history, so many fire-
souls. 133 they estimate, tossed overboard, chains
as ballast, mid-ocean, to wander subterranean
caves and valleys, lost among drowned mountains,
fallacious plants seducing salt-blistered tongues.

The newspaper woman sold at the station
fetched £4,500: a buyer's market.
Living with her mother and two accidental children
in a coldwater Lithuanian tower block,
offered employment abroad, a free-market choice.
Transported. Entrained. Cattled. Raped.
'On average I had sex with 15 men a day.
When trade was brisk and the itch was hot
in the dermis of the city, I could service 37 during
a single 12-hour shift. I was not much beaten.'

'It's a matter of business,' said the pimp.
'The law of supply and demand.'

2

'How can the giver of gifts experience the delights of the merchant?'
WILLIAM BLAKE

Geology precedes economics as the winter tide
on a chalky southern shore
reseeds naked meadow-beaches with black stone.
Dumb repetition smoothes anger, making a palliative
fiction from crimes we choose to celebrate.
The cliffs of England, vertical boneyards,
'where the ebb meets the moon-blanch'd sand',
hide lists of scoured dead, unbranded, unaccounted.
They bleed pure water and look in preserved shipping manifests
like so many maggots freighting an iron surf-board.

Edinburgh was fortunate in its geology, martial
in dirk and kirk, a craggy extrusion of volcanic basalt:
garrison, royalty, prisoners of war buried in the rock.
Into the protected tail of sandstone, they dig,
invisibles, ragged imports, the necessary
collateral damage: child labourers, hunchback women,
wageless slaves. Every bridge a den, damp cellars
like hollowed skulls candled in human tallow.
'Boys were employed to sit far underground,
guarding the fire flaps that punctuated
the long dark tunnels. Even after reforms
passed into law, the conditions in the mines
remained little changed. Money was too cheap.'

3

'The slaves will sell their masters and grow wings.'

Better to buy than to breed: the riderless white horse,
its sounding ribs a wind-harp,
emerges from a crystal sea. A skeleton jockey
gilded braid, cherries and tassels, incubates
revolt, raises a flaming sword to crop melon-heads,
moon faces in a cane field, strong teeth ground down
for sacred sugar. John Gabriel Steadman, a mercenary,
publishes his *Narrative of a Five Years' Expedition Against
the Revolted Negroes of Surinam from the year 1772 to 1777*,
and hires the journeyman engraver, William Blake of London,
to harvest the fruit of horror, flesh barbecues,
blood-succoured tropical vegetation, amateur crucifixions.
And the 'beautiful mulatto slave girl', Joanna,
the one Steadman marries, mother of his child.

Torn by a dark tarot of images, the colonist keeps a journal
of his London visit: 'Gave a sugar cruse to Mrs Blake.
The King's coach insulted. Met 300 whores in the Strand.
French prisoners come home. Abershaw &c. hang'd.
Saw a mermaid. Russian fleet down. Two days at Blake's.
Quiberon expedition fail'd. 188 emigrants executed.
Blake mobb'd and robb'd.' The working artist, enslaved by
patronage, lays the first brick of the downriver factory.

The impulse is coded within our DNA, this slippery
hawser of genetic imperatives: to invade, brutalise,
capture and explain. Secret interior tribes, our memory,
are linked, neck to neck, for pilgrimages across desert.
They follow a malarial river to a red fort, hungry surf.
Remember: 'We come out of the ground.' The grace of
their bodies as they negotiate space is future war. Jungles
migrate. Hurts multiply. Trade is the only constant.

'By the late 1820s the economic critique of slave-grown
sugar had been widely accepted.' The system didn't pay.
Better to allow open competition and let fiscal malpractice
thrive where it would. Queen Elizabeth's slave-master,
Sir John Hawkins, the pirate, founded an alms house
at Chatham that still stands. The Thames remains
a complicated flow of money, letters of credit and
trading instructions. The Port of London authority
building with its fossils and steroidal statuary now deals
in re-insurance, risk, power breakfasts. Fixed profit.

'The slaves changed,' Brian Catling wrote, in an unpublished
late-surrealist novel, 'before the morals of their owners.
They had transformed into other beings. Beings devoid of
purpose, identity or meaning. At the beginning it was thought
that their malaise was the product of their imprisonment.
But it soon became clear that there was no personality left to
feel and suffer such a subtlety of emotion. It was the forest
itself that had devoured their memory and resurrected them
as addicts to trees.'

Chris Steele-Perkins

Slavery, in different forms, in different places, in different times links these photographs. In 1997, when I took the photograph of the garbage-collecting children in Karachi, I was not thinking of them as slaves, I was thinking of them as part of a process where waste is re-cycled, plastics, metals collected, sorted, melted down, transformed, re-used. A good thing.

Only later did I start to think about whether they had any choice in the matter, if they had other realistic options in order to survive, whether they were physically intimidated into doing what they do. I don't really know the answer, but why would anyone spend all day up to their necks in toxic filth if they did have a choice?

How toxic language too can be. Comfort Women. Soft, gentle words to disguise rape and unbridled cruelty. During the Pacific war the Japanese military systematically kidnapped girls and young women from the countries they occupied to be sex-slaves.

Those with the courage to speak out later in their lives provide extraordinary testimonies of brutality and survival. Even, as for Lee Yong Soo, the tragic echo of doomed love.

We don't know what slaves look like, because they look like us, they are some of us, many of us; they wear no shackles and chains, they are invisibly bound by heart and mind.

Chris Steele-Perkins

Children Scavenging in Karachi, 2009–10
Lithograph, 39.5 × 49 cm
Included in *de luxe* edition of *I Have Found a Song*

Lee Yong Soo (born 1928)

Lee Yong Soo came from a poor family whose mother worked as a nanny and whose father delivered rice. She was 16 when a friend called her out of the house to meet a Japanese man who gave her a dress and leather shoes and promised more if they came and worked for him. There were four other girls, including her friend, with the man and she was too excited to think about where they were going.

They travelled for several days to the north of Korea and were made to work harvesting radishes. The man's behaviour changed and he beat them if they made mistakes or complained.

After a month they were taken by a Japanese naval ship to Taiwan. The girls were repeatedly raped on the journey and Lee Yong Soo contracted a sexual disease.

There they were forced to work in a 'Comfort Station' where they had to have sex three or four times a day, even when they had periods. They were beaten and electrocuted if they resisted. They mainly had to service Kamikaze pilots before suicide missions. Lee Yong Soo was not allowed to speak Korean and given the name Doshiko. She was never paid.

One suicide pilot (whom she had sexually infected previously) fell in love with her and before his fatal mission came and gave her his final possessions: a photo and his toiletries. He told her the disease was a gift from her, Doshiko, to him. He was gentle and he taught her a song:

> Take off bravely. Leaving Shin-jook
> Crossing over the clouds
> There is no one to see me off
> Only one crying for me. Doshiko.

After the war was over she found her way home and her mother was frightened and thought she was a ghost, believing her dead.

She feels much better now she has revealed what happened to her as a sex slave. She has never married and lives alone.

CHRIS STEELE-PERKINS

Lee Sun Duk

She was 17 years old and working on a farm harvesting when she was taken by a Japanese soldier. She was put in a room with 15 other girls and then taken to Shanghai and made to work at a sex station. There she was frequently beaten for resisting and this has damaged her eyesight. She had to have sex every day of the year. When she finally came home both her parents had died.

Jang Jum Dol

She was 14 and on the way to do laundry when she was taken by a Japanese man and told she was going to a factory to make money, but she was tied up in a house with an 11-year-old girl and then taken with some other girls to Manchuria. She tried to escape and was captured and beaten and kept as at a sex station with a wire fence around it. She had three children there and two of them died; the surviving girl had a weak heart. She had to continue as a sex slave. When she came back to Korea with her daughter after the war she was so poor she had to sleep in the streets.

CHRIS STEELE-PERKINS

Kang Il-Chul (born 1928)

She was taken by a military police officer saying she was being conscripted for the National Guard. Instead she was taken to a sex station in China where she was raped until her vagina bled. Twice she attempted suicide. She is not interested in financial compensation but wants public acknowledgement by the Japanese.

In 2002 I did a story for *Der Spiegel* magazine about child trafficking inside Africa. In this case children from Togo were trafficked to other counties such as Gabon where they worked as slave labour predominately in households or for market traders.

A remarkable man, Baba Apoudjac, ran an NGO to try and return these children to their families in Togo. Is the girl with the green top a slave? I don't know. I had to sneak the photograph and could not ask her, and would she have dared to say if she was? Probably she was, according to Baba Apoudjac, for many of such children are. The trade still goes on.

The boy in fatigues with frightened eyes was a slave. Maybe he was 12 when I took this photograph in 1997. He had managed to escape after being abducted by The Lord's Resistance Army (LRA) and forced to become a killer. The LRA is a lunatic religious sect, then based in Southern Sudan, roaming parts of Acholi land in Northern Uganda, abducting children and raping and mutilating the local population. Legs, arms, lips, noses would be cut off.

They claimed that the Ten Commandments drove them.

Chris Steele-Perkins

Hugo Williams *The Boy-Call*

The long drawn-out cry
of 'Boy!' echoes from the stairwell,
travels down two flights
and bursts like a blow to the head
through the last door on the left,
where I am sitting struggling with my essay
on the American civil war.
Only Briggs is behind me in the scrum
of tailcoats and bumfreezers
jockeying for position in the corridor.
He gets hold of my tails
and whips me against the wall.

Church is standing at the top of the stairs,
looking down at me. He's wearing
a blue silk waistcoat with silver stars,
a clove carnation, braided tailcoat,
spongebag trousers with sixteen-inch bottoms.
He scribbles a note,
twists it into the usual flat knot
and chucks it down to me.
'Take this to Howe in Chamier's
and bring me the answer.'
As soon as I am out of sight
I duck into an alley and unfold the note.
'What do you think of this one?
See you in Tap after school.'
Howe isn't in, so I leave the note in Chamier's
and head for the record shop –
out of bounds to Lower Boys.

There is a knock on my door
and Church is standing there,
holding up a ten shilling note.
'Do you want to know what this is for, H. Williams?'
He wants me to go to Thomas's the hairdresser,
to buy a suitable cane
with which to be beaten. He gives me the money
and I take off once more
in the direction of the High Street.
At Thomas's I ask to see a selection
and the old gentleman takes down
various items for my approval:
the knobbly 'School' cane,
the curve-handled 'Pop' cane,
the straight but bendy 'House' cane.
I can't make up my mind!

After supper I am called to the 'Library',
a book-free zone,
plastered with nude pin-ups.
The House Debating Society
is sitting round on sofas,
pretending to read newspapers
with holes cut in them.
'Stop ogling the women, Williams.
You aren't here to enjoy yourself.'
Church conducts the proceedings,
flexing the cane I bought for him earlier.
'You were seen in O'Sullivan's Record Shop
dancing the Charleston.
Perhaps you'd care to demonstrate?'
He puts on 'Good Golly Miss Molly' by Little Richard
and I kick up my heels.
'All right, you can stop doing that.
Put your head under the table.'
He flicks up my tails with his cane,
takes aim with a little tap.
The whirr of air, the sudden punctuation mark.
And then the absorption, the storing away
of anything like tears or cries,
as if for later use.

Benjamin Zephaniah *An Interesting Visit*

On an errand for my master
I chanced upon a crowd,
Then I feared some dread disaster
For their speech was fierce and loud,
Gathered round a notice nailed
Upon a wall on Black Boy Yard,
I tried to read but failed
For then I found such tasks quite hard.

I was told by one who read well
That we all should celebrate,
But without much thought I could tell
Not all thought this news so great,
There was cursing, spit, and anger
I saw happiness in some,
Some were warning of much danger
Some thought better was to come.

Then the literate one told me
'Be proud young African,
Equiano is now free
And he shall visit Birmingham,
From a slave to man of letters
He hath written to inform
Humble persons and law setters
Of hard times since he was born.'

I was filled with great excitement
I was overcome with joy,
Me thoughts Equiano was God sent
Working in great God's employ,
I had heard of his great travels
Word had spread of his wise plan
To rid us of all our travails
And help free his fellow man.

The year was seventeen ninety
As midsummer spread its sun,
For a month I waited patiently
For the gentleman to come,
To debate with Matthew Boulton
Joseph Priestley and James Watt,
To share with men of vision
And to challenge who hath not.

Pray let me tell of Birmingham
Its conflicts, joys and pains,
Fit for revolution
But still making slavery's chains,
Some strong women of this city
Did boycott the sugar trade,
Whilst other people with less pity
Cared not how their wealth was made.

A humble servant then was I
Owned by a wealthy trader
Who gained me as a real cheap buy
But claimed he was no slaver,
He christened me with new name
And though he hath not beat me
His ears were deaf to my claim
That Christ wants us to live free.

And so I prayed much and I waited
With ripe anticipation,
As people on the streets debated
Law and abolition,
Then with the visit nearing
My master raged and made me low
For with his lack of caring
He forbad me to go.

My anger had not measure
In my veins my blood brew hot,
I felt a rising pressure
My inner head did hurt a lot,
I reasoned and I pleaded
As if to beg for my survival,
Although some compromise was needed
My master said his word was final.

So when Equiano came
I was subject to harsh restrictions,
My master felt no shame
Yet he was full of contradictions,
In his view I was fortunate
And my suffering could be greater,
He thought Equiano full of hate,
An ungrateful troublemaker.

But yea, although my hero
Came and walked in my city,
I have no doubt – I do know
He communicates with me,
I heard of great words spoken by him
And those words planted a seed,
That well-sown seed has grown and risen
And yea, I taught myself to read.

That's how I read his narrative
That's how he came to me,
Inspired by his will to live
I too made myself free,
When Equiano came to Birmingham
The town's foundations shook,
No force can stop Equiano and
The truth and power of his book.

Artist Biographies

Sonia Dawn Boyce was born in London in 1962 and emerged in the early 1980s as a figurative painter, gaining critical attention as an emerging figure in the black British arts movement for works that spoke about racial identity and gender in contemporary Britain. She has exhibited in: *Century City – art and culture in the modern metropolis*, Tate Modern (2001); *Devotional*, National Portrait Gallery, London (2007); *Crop Over*, Harewood House, Leeds and Barbados National Museum (2007–8); *For you, only you*, Oxford University and tour (2007-8); *Menschen und Orte*, Kunstverein Konstanz, Constance (2008); *Praxis – art in times of uncertainty*, Thessaloniki Biennale of Contemporary Art (2009); *Like Love – 1, 2 and 3*, Spike Island, Bristol, and tour (2009–10). She is currently an AHRC Research Fellow at Wimbledon College of Art and Design, University of the Arts.

Hew Locke was born in Edinburgh, raised in Guyana, and lives in London. Recently he has been exploring visual projections of power – as used both by nations and by individuals. He celebrates global cultural fusions, creating complex sculptures with an eclectic range of objects including mass produced consumer detritus. Locke has exhibited extensively within the UK, including solo shows at the V&A, The New Art Gallery in Walsall, Chisenhale Gallery and Rivington Place. In the USA he has had solo shows at the Luckman Gallery LA and Atlanta Contemporary Arts. His work is in many public collections, including the Arts Council of England, British Museum, Brooklyn Museum, Government Art Collection, Henry Moore Institute, Kemper Museum of Contemporary Art, Tate Gallery, and Victoria & Albert Museum.

Shanti Panchal was born in Mesar, India, and came to England on a British Council scholarship to study at the Byam Shaw School of Art. He has been artist-in-residence at the British Museum, the Harris Museum in Preston, and the Winsor & Newton Art Factory in London, and has had solo shows at Cartwright Hall, Bradford; Royal Festival Hall, London; Museum of Modern Art, Oxford; Midlands Arts Centre, Birmingham; Chelmsford Museum; and a British Council tour to India in 2003 entitled *Shanti Panchal: a Personal Journey.* He has been a prizewinner in the John Moores Liverpool Exhibition, the BP Portrait Awards and won first prize in the Singer & Friedlander/*Sunday Times* watercolour competition. His work is in many public collections, including the Arts Council, Birmingham Museum and Art Gallery, Imperial War Museum and the Walker Art Gallery, Liverpool.

Paula Rego was born in Portugal and studied in London at the Slade School of Art, where she met the artist Victor Willing, whom she later married. She is widely acclaimed as one of the leading figurative artists in the world, celebrated in particular for her pastels and prints. She has had many solo exhibitions, including retrospectives at the Gulbenkian in Lisbon, the Serpentine Gallery, Tate Liverpool, the Serralves Museum in Oporto, Tate Britain, the Reina Sofia in Madrid, and the National Museum of Women in the Arts, Washington DC. In September 2009, the Casa das Histórias Paula Rego, a new museum dedicated to her work, was inaugurated at Cascais in Portugal. Paula Rego was the first National Gallery Associate Artist, and holds honorary doctorates from the universities of St Andrews, East Anglia, Roehampton and Oxford.

Chris Steele-Perkins' early work as a photographer was largely concerned with urban poverty and subcultures in Britain. In 1979 he published his first solo book, *The Ted*, documenting the myth of the Teddy Boy. In the same year he joined Magnum Photos and began working in the developing world, particularly in Africa, Central America and Lebanon, as well as continuing to document Britain. In 1992 he published *Afghanistan* and in 2000 the first of his photographic explorations of Japan, *Fuji*, which was followed in 2006 by *Tokyo Love Hello*. His book *Northern Exposures* (2006) documents rural life in Durham. His work was included in the Arts Council Collection exhibition and book *No Such Thing as Society: Photography in Britain 1967–87* (2007) and the Hayward Gallery's touring exhibition *Disposable People: Contemporary Global Slavery* (2008–9).

Writer Biographies

Patience Agbabi is a poet, performer and Fellow in Creative Writing at Oxford Brookes University. She has worked extensively with the British Council and performed her work all over the world. In 2004 she was nominated one of the UK's Next Generation Poets. Her latest collections are *Transformatrix* (Canongate, 2000) and *Bloodshot Monochrome* (Canongate, 2008). She is currently Canterbury Laureate and has recently received a Grant for the Arts to support a forthcoming collection based on *The Canterbury Tales*.

Polly Atkin was born in Nottingham, lived in East London for seven years, and is now based in Cumbria. She is currently researching the construction of meaning around place for a PhD in English and Sociology at the University of Lancaster, under the AHRC's Landscape and Environment Scheme. Her pamphlet *Bone Song* was published in 2008.

Valerie Bloom was born in Clarendon, Jamaica and came to England in 1974. She gained a first in English with African and Caribbean Studies at the University of Kent. She has written a number of poetry collections and two novels, run writing courses for the Arvon Foundation, led workshops for students, teachers and librarians and has had residencies worldwide. She has performed her work at festivals, on television and radio in Britain, Europe, Africa and the Caribbean. She writes poetry in both English and in Jamaican patois for readers of all ages. She currently lives in Kent with her husband and three children.

Jean 'Binta' Breeze is a writer and performer of international standing. An artist with a strong sense of place, she grew up in rural Jamaica and then lived and worked in Kingston, where she soon established herself as a key writer, performer and recording artist. Her most recent books are *The Arrival of Brighteye and Other Poems* (2000) and *The Fifth Figure: A Poet's Tale* (2006).

Fred D'Aguiar was born in London to Guyanese parents and grew up in Guyana. He trained as a psychiatric nurse before reading African and Caribbean Studies at the University of Kent. He has published five collections of poetry, including *Bill of Rights* (1998; shortlisted for the T. S. Eliot Prize) and *An English Sampler: New and Selected Poems* (2001). D'Aguiar is also a playwright and novelist. He is currently Professor of English and Gloria D. Smith Professor of Africana Studies at Virginia Tech State University, USA. His most recent collection *Continental Shelf*, was shortlisted for the 2009 T. S. Eliot Prize.

Helen Dunmore is a poet, novelist, children's writer and short story writer. Her latest collection of poems is *Glad of These Times* (Bloodaxe, 2007), and her new novel is *The Betrayal* (Fig Tree), published in spring 2010. She was the inaugural winner of the Orange Prize for Fiction, and among other prizes has won the McKitterick Prize, The Signal Award for Poetry, and the Alice Hunt Bartlett Award. Her work is translated into more than twenty-five languages. She is a Fellow of the Royal Society of Literature.

Paul Farley has published three books of poetry to widespread acclaim and received many awards, including the Forward Prize, the Somerset Maugham Award, and in 1999 he was named the *Sunday Times Young Writer of the Year*. He has also written a study of Terence Davies' *Distant Voices, Still Lives*, and edited a *Selected* John Clare. He works as a teacher, freelance writer and broadcaster, and lives in north Lancashire.

Bernardine Evaristo is the author of two critically-acclaimed novels-in-verse: *Lara* (1997) and *The Emperor's Babe* (2001) and one novel-with-verse, *Soul Tourists* (2005). She has undertaken over 50 international writers' tours since 1997, and has been a visiting professor at Barnard College/Columbia University in New York, writer-in-residence at the University of the Western Cape, Cape Town, and writing fellow at the University of East Anglia and is a Fellow of the Royal Society of Literature and the Royal Society of Arts. Her novel *Blonde Roots* (Penguin, 2008) is an imaginative inversion of the transatlantic slave trade in which Africans are the masters and Europeans are the slaves.

Jacob Sam-La Rose is a poet, educator and editor. A touring poet with the British Council, his debut pamphlet *Communion* was selected as the Poetry Book Society Choice for Autumn 2006. He manages a range of youth poetry initiatives, including www.thefoundryproject.org and the London Teenage Poetry SLAM.

Iain Sinclair has lived in (and written about) Hackney, East London, since 1969. His novels include *Downriver* (winner of the James Tait Black Prize and the Encore Prize for the year's best second novel), *Radon Daughters*, *Landor's Tower* and, most recently, *Dining on Stones* (which was shortlisted for the Ondaatje prize). Non-fiction works include *Lights Out for the Territory*, *London Orbital* and *Edge of the Orison*. He has also written and presented films for BBC2's *Late Show* and co-directed four documentaries for Channel 4. One of these, *Asylum*, won the short film prize at the Montreal Festival. His most recent book, *Hackney, That Rose-Red Empire*, was published in 2009.

Hugo Williams won the T. S. Eliot Prize for his 1999 collection, *Billy's Rain*. *Dear Room* (2006) was shortlisted for the Costa Poetry Prize. His latest collection, *West End Final*, was shortlisted for the 2009 T. S. Eliot Prize. He is the poetry editor of the *New Statesman*, and was recently awarded the Queen's Gold Medal for Poetry.

Benjamin Zephaniah was born in Birmingham, England. His first book of poems, *Pen Rhythm*, was published in 1980 and he has published a further 11 works and 12 recordings. His work has inspired a new generation of artists from writers, rappers and performance poets. Benjamin Zephaniah hosted Nelson Mandela's Two Nations Concert at the Royal Albert Hall in July 1996. He has acquired 13 honorary doctorates in acknowledgement of his work and a wing in a West London hospital has been named after him.

I Have Found a Song has been designed
by Peter Willberg and printed in Verona
by Editoriale Bortolazzi Stei.
It is set in Collis and Gothic 720 and printed
on 150 gsm GardaPat Kiara with Aniva inks.

The *de luxe* edition consists of thirty-five copies
numbered 1/35 to 35/35, five *hors commerce* copies
numbered HC 1/5 to 5/5, and six publisher's
copies numbered i/vi to vi/vi.

In addition there are ten artist's proofs of each
original print, numbered AP 1/10 to AP 10/10.
The etchings by Sonia Boyce and Paula Rego and
lithographs by Hew Locke and Chris Steele-Perkins
have been printed on 300 gsm Somerset White at
Paupers Press, and Shanti Panchal's ink-jet print
has been printed on 315 gsm Da Vinci Soft Textured
at Chaudigital.

The *de luxe* edition has been bound and slipcased
by The Fine Book Bindery.

The regular edition consists of 350 casebound copies.